# HOW TO IDENTIFY AND AVOID A NO GOOD

# SKEEZER

J. DUVAL

Marvin,
Best wishes to you!!!
Jai Duval
4/14/2016

The

Good Man's

Survival Guide

# HOW TO IDENTIFY AND AVOID A NO GOOD SKEEZER

(Second Edition)

J. DUVAL

LOS ANGELES, CALIFORNIA

P.O. Box 91261

Los Angeles, California 90009

Email: jduvalseries@yahoo.com



Printed and Bound in the United States of America

Published and Distributed by:

KATSUDO Publishing

P.O. Box 91261

Los Angeles, CA 90009

(310) 927-1987

Email: katsudopublishing@yahoo.com

Cover Layout by Kevin Allen

Graphic Images by Afrocentrix

The text book is composed in 12 pt., Verdana font

PUBLISHER'S NOTE:

This is a work of fiction. Names, characters, organizations, places, and incidents either are the product of the author's imagination <u>or</u> are used fictitiously, and any

resemblance to actual persons, living or dead, business establishments, organizations, events, or locales is entirely coincidental.

Library of Congress Cataloging-in-Publication Data

Duval, J.

**The Good Man's Survival Guide – How to Identify and Avoid a No Good Skeezer**

**Quote:**

~~~~~~

*"It is better to be*

*Informed, Happy and Available*

*than to be*

*Ignorant, Unhappy and Stuck*

*with a Skeezer"*

~~~~~~

- J. Duval

# TABLE OF CONTENTS

## Acknowledgements

My deepest regrets go out to those good men who have suffered emotionally, physically, financially and are still suffering today from their own foolish behavior and the scandalous behavior of those no good skeezers.

I realize some men will never recover emotionally or financially in their lifetime which include those in marital and non-marital relationships. I use their unhappy situations as a template to establish what you should not want in your life, what you should refuse to accept and what you should never have in any of your relationships.

I thank God that I was never that severely beaten down and experienced only disappointment rather than emotional and financial pain and suffering.

I want to thank all of the good women whom I have met over the years because if it not for you, I would not have known the difference between a good woman and a no good skeezer and I too might have been beaten down and/or stuck.

Finally, I want to thank all of you skeezers I came in contact with over the years because if not for you, this guide to assist good men to hopefully avoid your scandalous asses would not exist.

## Introduction

This guide is based upon years of experience, observation and testimonials and is to be used to assist good men in eliminating skeezers that not only use them but ruin the opportunity for good women to establish healthy relationships as well.

Where are most of the good men? They have been programmed by today's society and have allowed themselves to be held captive physically, emotionally and financially by abusive, lying, inconsiderate and irresponsible skeezers that are pretending to be good women.

What happen? They evolved over a couple of generations into what is called the gentleman.

What is a gentleman? A gentleman is a good man that has willingly surrendered his dignity, trained to believe that his life is worthless unless he has a woman living with him and he is doing everything that he can to please her regardless of any potential harmful impact to him.

His duties (or existence) consist primarily of:

A. Protect, serve and obey her without thought
B. Lie and tell her what she wants to hear
C. Give her whatever she wants to shut her up
D. Think like a slave by doing the most and expecting the least
E. Solicit prostitution from her (sex or household duties in exchange for cash, clothing, jewelry, vacations, expensive dining, paying her bills.)
F. Accept physical, verbal and financial abuse from her and consider that as being a man.
G. Reduce his self-worth by having to prove his worthiness without requiring the same of her

This does not represent every good man although it does represent the majority of good men that have sacrificed the pursuit of prosperity and peace-of-mind for a no good skeezer.

The good women know who these skeezers are because a lot of them are their closest friends. They envy their skeezing friends because of the attention and benefits that their friends are receiving and they still won't expose them. By accepting and not exposing those skeezers, the good women allow skeezers to destroy the possibility for them and other good women to establish a meaningful relationship.

To the good men that aren't held captive, this guide will assist you in recognizing and avoiding the majority of skeezers and increase your chances of a peaceful and prosperous life. The key is avoiding them once you recognize them.

This guide is not for the Players because they are in complete control of the women they interact with and aren't looking for a commitment. They are simply looking for a good time and know that there are more than their share women that will accommodate them.

# Chapter 1 - What is a SuckerMan?

SuckerMan is helpful, nice and a hopeless fool.

A. He allows her to tell him what to do

B. He allows her to take advantage of his interest in her by having him take her places, run errands and repair things for her at no charge he listens to her complaints about other men

C. He is always available for her emotionally, physically and financially but she isn't for him

D. He knows she isn't interested but he hangs around hoping she will change her mind

E. He never gets the booty and she knows he never will but may constantly tease him to keep him around and hoping

F. She constantly reminds him of what a good friend he is whenever he tries to get

PHYSICALLY too close to her

## Chapter 2 - What is a Skeezer?

A skeezer is a selfish, inconsiderate female that takes advantage of a male's time, resources and finances due to his personal interest in her.

There is no exterior appearance that defines a skeezer which makes them quite difficult to recognize. They vary in size, color and class so you have to recognize her by her attitude and behavior.

A skeezer will impersonate, with fraudulent intent, the character of a good woman so she can prey (not pray) on and use good men to support her selfish, irresponsible and inappropriate lifestyle.

Skeezers will also use their children or get pregnant if they have to. There are no limits to what a skeezer will do to get what she wants regardless of the damaging impact to her male victims or her children.

## Chapter 3 - How to Flip the Script on a Skeezer

The vast majority of women are taking advantage of decent males that have a personal interest in them. A considerate and unselfish woman would not accept you spending your money feeding or entertaining her **IF** she has no genuine interest in you. She would be considerate and pay her own way in that case to be fair and keep it platonic.

Since the majority of both sexes are conditioned to go the traditional route where the man invites and pays during the dating process, I suggest that males following my **2 DATE SCREENING RULE**.

Date 1 - Coffee Shop: Meet her, not pick her up, at a coffee shop so that you spend more time getting to know her as opposed to spending more money. If you get bad vibes about her during that time you have only spent a few bucks and you are done with her. If the first date goes well look into her eyes and ask if she would like to meet you for breakfast or lunch. If she moves her eyes away from yours and seem a bit hesitant she is not feeling you so don't persist and consider this your first and last date with her.

Date 2 - Breakfast or Lunch: Again meet her and don't pick her up. Never meet a woman for dinner or some form of entertainment on the second date because of the cost and secondly her attention will be on the entertainment and not you. These kinds of events you reserve for someone that has displayed a genuine interest in you. Again, pay for the date (because she expects you to do so) but make sure you keep it to a minimum. Don't think that just because she is there that she is genuinely interested in you. Remember, you are paying and skeezers typically will **NEVER REFUSE A FREE MEAL**. During that second date you want to know how her schedule is so include some of that in the conversation as a discovery process (the importance of it will come later). If she says that she is a very busy person and don't say that she can make time to spend with you then this will be your last date with her. At the end of the second date, get ready to now expose her intentions by following the script below:

You Say - *"Hey, I think these have been a couple of pretty good dates. What do you think?"* (Say nothing else and wait for her response. If she does not agree then you are done with her. If she does agree, which most will regardless, that's when you pop the **BIG** question).

You Say - *"So when are you going to invite me out on a date?"* (This is where the information about how busy her schedule comes in to play. If she did not state that she was very busy then she should have no problem inviting you out **UNLESS** she really doesn't give a crap about you. If she says she isn't sure then you now know she has no genuine interest in you because she stated earlier that she was not that busy of a person.

**NOTE**: **DO NOT** be a whiner and say, "*well, you said earlier that you were not that busy*". Just accept it as a small price to pay to identify a skeezer and don't see, talk to or cater to her again. She does not have to know why you no longer want to see her because she is not being genuine with you. This shows you that she is just killing time with you.

There are some women accustomed to expensive dining and will expect you to bear the expenses if you want to dine with them. If you are a weak male, I would say avoid these types and leave them to the players and dogs who know how to run the proper game on them or males (with balls) who know how to simply say **NO** to them. I would suggest that this tactic be used on any woman that a male is not sure of her true intentions.

Here's a tip on identifying a woman that has no respect for you and is just killing time and/or looking for an opportunity to get you to spend your money on her.  How are you going to know that in advance? In most cases, the majority of average males will not know so I suggest that they proceed with caution.  A female that values you and has a genuine interest in you will not try to get a free ride off of you. If she is not interested in you, she will know before the date is over and she should pay her own way because she knows you are doing so due to a personal interest in her and not just to spend money. Then again, she would have to be a thoughtful and considerate person which many of them aren't.

The following tactic should be used to determine if a female has a genuine interest in you or is only using you to kill time and get a free meal. This would have to be done at a sit-in restaurant where you pay after the meal is finished. Remember, you won't know her intentions until you get her to a restaurant and ask her the right question.

1. Agree to meet at a restaurant. Do not pick her up and do not mention paying for the date.

2. When you get the menu and are ready to order, "let her order for herself" (this is very

important)

3. Let the conversation flow and at some point just prior to the meal being paid for look her directly in her eyes and ask, "Would you like to get together again? If so, will you pick up the next tab"? Do not say another word until she gives you an answer and if she asks you to repeat what you said; say exactly the same thing. Don't change the conversation. If she resists responding to your question, says she doesn't want to see you again or says that she doesn't believe a woman should pay, simply pay your portion and not hers. You are being used as a sucker (i.e. fool). The restaurant cannot make you pay for her because you did not order for her.

4. After you pay your portion offer to walk her to her car and if she says no just walk away from her and consider yourself fortunate that you weren't another one of her suckers. See it as a victory because you had an opportunity to get out, you had a nice meal, you only paid for yourself and you've learned how to identify and

flip the script on a skeezer.

Many will consider this tactic cruel and scandalous but if she has no personal interest in you she should state that. Trust me, they know if they are physically attracted to you and have a personal interest. If she isn't interested in you and will not tell you or will not pay for her portion of the date then she has no respect for you. Any tactic you use on her, before she uses you, is justified. Do not let those weak males out there tell you otherwise.

**FINALLY:** If you are going to pay for the date you should **NEVER** allow her to tell you where she wants to go. You make that determination because you are the one paying. Don't be **STUPID** and a **FOOL**.

## Chapter 4 - How to Suppress that Skeezer Urge in Her

Has she gotten on your last nerve? Do you feel stuck or trapped? The next time you notice that skeezer coming out of her, give her some of your **A.S.S.** to temporarily suppress her. There is no known cure for that inconsiderate attitude yet so until then, "Get some A.S.S. to save your ass".

## Chapter 5 - Good Men Aren't Valued, Good Men Are Used

Your first impression will be a lasting impression. If you begin behaving foolishly trying to impress an unproven woman by spending money, buying gifts and doing things for her you will have to continue to behave in that manner. She is not looking at your character she is looking at what she can get out of you. Once she has gotten all she can you are out and the next suckerman is in.

Many good men have been socially conditioned to simply protect and serve any woman he has an interest in while many of those same women will protect and serve a man that has no genuine interest in them.

When a man speaks the truth about lazy, no good women he is considered angry and bitter. When a woman speaks the truth about lazy, no good men she is praised for speaking out and letting other women know about these types of men. Why is that? The answer is because most men aren't valued beyond their finances or deeds and they have been socially conditioned to think they are to do whatever it takes to get and please a woman regardless of the consequences to themselves.

Most women don't want a good man; they want instant gratification and fantasy. They want a man that will support their irresponsible past and present behavior. They also want a man that will fulfill their romantic fantasy of continuous wining, dining and freely spending his money on them. What they don't seem to or want to realize is that certain personalities are usually associated with that behavior. Here are 3 of those personalities:

Controlling – He spends his money on them and he wants them available to him when needed. He spends the cash so he calls the shots.

Insecure – He feels as if he has to spend money or buy them things to be with them. He has a very low level of self-esteem and for whatever reason has problems attracting women that he has a genuine interest in and is attracted to.

Ladies Man – He is secure with himself and is accustomed to spending money on women and enjoying their company. He has no problem spending money and does it on a regular basis. He will never be monogamous because he thrives off of having access to multiple women.

These men are neither right nor wrong, they are simply who they are. Good women choose them, try to change them, pray or hope eventually they will change and be monogamous with just them.

They will never separate their spending from the personality because it's a packaged deal.

If a woman wants a good, honest, responsible man that's not expecting her to financially support him then she should behave like a good, honest and responsible woman that's not expecting him to financially support her. In other words, she should reflect in herself that behavior which she wants and expects out of a man. The next chapter describes some qualities of a good woman that you can use to assist in your selection.

## Chapter 6 - Is She a Good Woman or Just a Skeezer?

Some women have no clue what a good woman is because most men either don't know or don't tell them. Here are some basic qualities that any woman can and should consistently display. These should be her minimum requirements.

1. She is emotionally healthy and free from past relationships.

2. She is seeking companionship to enhance her happiness and not to make her happy.

3. She is responsible and will not expect you to rescue her from drama or debt she creates.

4. She can sensibly communicate when angry and will not become a public embarrassment.

5. She comes to you first with personal issues or disagreements that the two of you may have.

6. She is happy being in a relationship with you without expecting you to entertain her all the time.

7. She can be content at home and does not

have to run the streets in order to be happy.

8. She accepts you and does not try to change you.

## Chapter 7 - Potential Mate Value (PMV) Chart

This applies only to females that consider themselves single, available and unattached.

Female's rate you based upon their criteria so it's time for you to start rating them in a manner that will benefit you. The PMV chart can be used as your baseline. You may modify the list to meet your personal preference since you will determine what an acceptable score is. Don't be too lenient in your scoring because trust me when I say that they aren't for you.

IMPORTANT NOTE: Just as points are deducted, she can receive rebates as well. For example, if she has 2 children at home, 2 point are deducted and her PMV drops by 2 points. Once the children are grown and out of the house, she receives 2 rebates and her PMV increases by 2 points. She can receive rebates in every category except for "age" unless, that is, she can reverse time.

| Category | Explanation | Points Taken Away |
|---|---|---|
| Age | As age increases, so does her willingness to become inflexible with a man. Deduct 1 point for every 5 years above the age of 30. (Ex.:35 =1, 40=2, etc.) | |
| Attitude | Selfish and inconsiderate when interacting with you. She does not value you and expects you to do most (if not all) of the planning. initiating contact with you and paying. Deduct 1 point | |
| Children | You will never come first as long as there is a child in the home. Deduct 1 point for each child in the home. | |
| Domestic Skills | She has no domestic skills. She can't cook, not organized and dines out most of the time. Deduct 1 point. | |
| Emotional Liability | She is not emotionally free. She is attached to someone in her past and refuses to let go. Deduct 1 point. | |

| | | |
|---|---|---|
| Financial Liability | Bad credit and does not pay bills on time, financially over-extended and living beyond her means. Deduct 1 point. | |
| Geographically Undesirable | Lives too far from you. Cannot see her other on a regular basis or at a moment's notice. Deduct 1 point. | |
| Physically Unavailable | Too busy (or pretends to be too busy) when it comes to spending time with you. It does not matter what the reason is because you can't get to know her if she is unavailable.<br>Deduct 1 point. | |
| Unemployed | She does not have a steady job or any steady source of income (child support or alimony excluded). She expects for you to put out more effort and money just because you have it to satisfy her own unreasonable and selfish expectations. Deduct 1point. | |
| | Total Point Deducted (TPD) → | |
| PMV | 10 (Top Score) - TPD = | |

Her PMV score will be ten which is a perfect score given to every female to begin with minus those deductions from the chart.

I purposely chose to not include her physical appearance since I've noticed you all have your own standards and personal preferences when it comes to what you consider attractive to be.

Remember that in this society we live in women rate you based upon your physical appearance, financial or social status such as where you live, if you own a home, how much money you make, how much of that money you spend on her or her children, how much of her responsibilities or pressure you place on your back or what benefit you can be to her so why should you be stupid and not rate her?

WARNING: Never mention to any woman that you are rating her based upon this chart. To do so would be a foolish and costly mistake.

## Chapter 8 - "DeAr" Hunting Season

**Pre-Season** - September 6th - October 30th

**Question:** What is De**A**r Hunting Season?

**Answer:** This is the time of year when many females will allow males of her choosing to spend "spend time with" and "spend money on" them.

If you have a good woman hold on to her because there are not many of them left. A good woman will not expect or require your financial support to be the glue that keeps the two of you together. If she does expect your finances to help maintain her lifestyle and happiness, you have a business arrangement with a woman whose services are for sale. I would suggest if she expects you to spend money on her, do so with no emotional attachment. See it for what it is which is a temporary, non-emotional business arrangement until you acquire a good woman or a less expensive business arrangement.

It's about the gift of giving and their self-esteem uplifting (at your expense of course) with the majority of them regardless of what they may say. Many females do not care about males or their financial well-being and it will be proven by her expectations to receive gifts and money regardless of the male's own personal financial responsibilities.

Many males will "again" go down in flames financially as they run to the malls and simply surrender their finances hoping to be successful and not be stressed out during DeAr Hunting season. I can only provide males with information to protect themselves but this information is useless if not applied.

If she genuinely cares she will tell him to not

spend his money on her knowing how bad the economy is. Many males will not have the balls to tell her that he will be spending less money on her this season and just spending quality time with her instead.

**PRE-SEASON**: September 6th - October 30th

Time to set a few traps and get in a little practice. This will keep your skills sharp and prepare you for the upcoming season. It's important to practice your offense as well as your defense.

The quality of DeAr is not as important as the quantity so get as much practice on as many DeAr as you can during pre-season. As you get closer to regular season start selecting DeAr that meets with your desired requirements. Many good men tend to stumble or freeze when they come in contact with a desirable DeAr due to lack of experience therefore practice is mandatory to gain that experience.

Beware of Poachers - Check traps on a regular basis·because poachers will attempt to steal your DeAr that is caught in one of your emotional traps and is vulnerable.

**REGULAR SEASON**: Oct 31st - Feb 14th

The DeAr will allow you to approach them due to their desire for gifts and attention. Don't be tricked into believing just because she allows you in that she genuinely cares for you.

**1st Quarter** (October 31st - November 30$^{th}$)

The first official day is extremely important and you should be out there if at all possible. Why this day? Because it's Halloween and they tend to let their guards down, be open to approach and act out those inhibitions they have been suppressing during the post-season. This is the day, at parties especially, that they feel the rush of the season coming on and you have to take full advantage of it. You should have your game face on and you should be out there hunting.

Don’t think about it, just go out and do it!!

**2nd Quarter** (December 1st - December 24$^{th}$)

By now you should be reaping the rewards of your traps because it's getting close to you know what (ho, ho, ho...). Choose that DeAr wisely because they are looking for gifts and someone to be with due to the seasonal pressure. They may not be interested in you initially and just caught up in all of the seasonal hype so take advantage of it.

**Halftime** (Christmas)

*"If Santa doesn’t come on Christmas morning, you definitely won’t come Christmas evening".*

Well, not with her and I am sure you know what I mean.

Do you have any money left? Were you stupid and spent lots of your money on her and received an inequitable exchange in return, maybe a "hug and kiss on the cheek" or a "tongue-less kiss on the lips" to keep you around? If so there is no hope for you so cut your losses, simply quit before you lose more money and wait until next season.

**3rd Quarter** (December 26th - January 15th)

This is the time to trap that DeAr that ignored you during the first half of the season. They probably missed out on that Christmas companionship, those Christmas gifts and now refuse to wait on the sidelines for him (usually a married man or a man already in a relationship) any longer. They will want to make sure that they are not left out on Valentine's Day. Get rid of the DeAr that you trapped during the first half of the season and have not mounted that is a liability to you and make room for new prospects.

**4th Quarter** (January 16th - February 14th)

This is your last chance to have a successful season if you haven't already been successful. If you have not trapped any DeAr by now you have to make your traps more desirable (i.e., do as most of those DeAr do to get your service which is use dishonesty and/or deceit) or lower your DeAr requirements so that you can end the season with at least one capture.

The Holy Day, Super Bowl Sunday is an excellent day to hunt and there is always an abundance of DeAr at the right parties. They tend to group together so you have to show no fear of rejection or weakness in your attempt at breaking one away from the herd.

**SUDDEN DEATH OVERTIME** (*Valentine's Day*): The final official day, the second most stressful day and the final opportunity of the season. The good man has been allowed, during the season, to spend time with her and more importantly spend money on her and he has now become emotionally attached. He wants to pop the commitment question but knows, "*I Love Her and She Loves Me Not*".

**POST SEASON:** February 15th - September 5th Termination Notification Time **(TNT).** This is the time many females prepare to issue termination notices to the good men they suckered during the season. They have received enough attention, money, gifts and a huge self-esteem boost to last them throughout the post season. Notices to their victims are similar to the one below:

*"Sweetie, thank you for the gifts, dinners and time we spent together these past few months. You've been a nice friend, a gentleman and a God sent blessing. Did I tell you that my ex and I are getting back together? or Did I tell you I met someone? He is very jealous and would not like me spending time with another man. I am sure you will find that special someone that will make your life complete. Thanks again for everything.* ***WE*** *wish you the best".*

The sad part about the whole ordeal is that most good men will never change their behavior and will get used again during the post-season and regular seasons to come. There will even be cases that the same skeezer that terminated him will recall him after she has been dumped just before the season starts again and those same foolish men will be more than willing to go back and cater to those skeezers again.

Post Season Blues **(PSB).** This is the time when many good men (suckermen) will enter that state of loneliness and depression after being served their termination notice. They will have been stripped of their self-esteem and money.

This is the time to repair any damages, relax, bond with other successful hunters, exchange experiences and share locations and ideas.

After a few months you need to begin preparation in any manner (financially, emotionally, and physically) for the next season.

**DO NOT** put forth any extra effort on DeAr you come in contact with during the post-season. **DO NOT** cater to any DeAr you did not mount during the previous season. Use minimal effort during the post-season on them and maximum effort on getting you prepared for the next season. Many of those post-season DeAr are bitter because they were used by the men they chose and dumped afterwards so save the effort, time and expense for the regular season.

## Chapter 9 - If You Pay, Have It Your Way

I am sure that many of us are guilty of doing what I am about to say. You see a female you are attracted to and she finds you physically appealing so she will allow you into her space and the opportunity to sell yourself.

Eventually, if you have the courage, you will ask her out on a dining date. I said dining because that is the common place males will invite a female. Most females will not say no to a meal if they feel comfortable with you. That level of comfort can range from them being physically attracted to you or knowing that they will have complete control of you and the situation even though they are not physically attracted to you.

I have been guilty of the following, in my distant past, and I am sure that other males have been as well. You ask her out, she says yes and then you ask her where would she like to go? **STOP RIGHT THERE!!!**

Never, ever ask a female where she would like to go if you are going to pay for the date. This is how females get the chance to eat at expensive places knowing that you will pay for it. If you are going to be spending your money then you are going to decide where to spend it.

If she sees you as a suckerman that is desperate for a date with her, she is going to try and get you to take her on as an expensive date as she can. She will even have you thinking that this will impress her. Well, I have to agree that you will impress her but for a totally different reason than you what you are thinking.

You will be impressing (showing) her how weak and easy you are for her to get you to do what she wants. They get offended or have very little patience for the man they are not attracted if he does not do what she wants. If this happens then she's not into you.

You need to have a place or places in mind before you ask her out on a dining date. If she asks where you are going to be taking her go ahead and tell her. When you tell her where you are going to take her don't ask her, "Is that place ok with you"? As long as the place is clean, safe and she likes you it will not matter to her.

Do not feel special because she allowed you to spend your money on her. If you have to spend your money on her to spend time with her she does not value you as a person anyway. Whether it is dining or some other social event, make sure that you decide whether you want her undivided attention if you are going to pay. After all, if you are going to pay for the time to be with her then don't allow her to enjoy that benefit without you have exclusive rights to that time.

# Chapter 10 - Whoso Findeth a Wife Findeth a Good Thing

*"I do willingly promise to comply with the laws that govern incarceration and prostitution and promise to provide compensation* ***IN HOPES*** *of receiving sexual and household services. I understand there will be many times when I will*

*not receive those services, will have to accept it, pretend to be happy and/or seek those services outside of this happy union"*.

That phrase, "Whoso Findeth a Wife..." is used quite often with women and most (not all) don't know what they are talking about.

You don't meet a woman and she automatically becomes your wife. If you are not swayed by her looks you should know that there is a process that you should follow before considering her as wife potential. I will move from the phrase backwards to help you out if you don't know.

A. Before she can become your wife she has to **CONSISTENTLY DISPLAY** wife-like qualities.

B. Before she can **DISPLAY** wife-like qualities she has to **KNOW** what those qualities are.

C. Before she can **KNOW** what those qualities are she has to **LEARN** those qualities.

D. The way to **LEARN** those qualities is to be **TAUGHT** by a knowledgeable, unselfish and sane male, female or group.

E. Before she can be **TAUGHT** those qualities she has to have the proper **ATTITUDE**.

Many females will have not been taught wife-like qualities. What most of them do know about being a wife was probably learned through direct observation at home which in many cases was occupied by a single parent, a not-so-healthy two parent situation or not-so-healthy mother and boyfriend household. Those households will typically consist of arguing, very little show of affection (touching, hugging or light kissing), irresponsible behavior and financial management and very little, if any, mature communication.

She may also have been negatively influenced by selfish and controlling women in dysfunctional relationships which typically look upon the man only as financial support, a handyman and/or a lifestyle upgrade. That man usually gives her what she wants to temporarily shut her up and maintain what he believes to be peace in that relationship. Those female types are usually never satisfied and the best thing he could do for himself is leave home and never return.

Until she can display those wife-like qualities on a consistent basis all you will have found is a thing. You don't know how good that thing is or if that thing can potentially become a loving wife and asset to the relationship or just another skeezer that will become a physical, emotional and financial burden.

Unless you are foolish you should never allow her to bring stress or debt into your life because she will expect you to help partially or totally bear her stress and financial burdens. Just being a female does not qualify her to be your wife.

If you don't have a clue what those wife-like qualities are then I suggest you return to the chapters, "Is She a Good Woman or just another Skeezer" and "Potential Mate Value (PMV) Chart" as your initial reference because if you aren't wise in your choices you will more than likely end up with a skeezer.

## Chapter 11 - Documented Skeezers

For the man that has NO productive goals in life and simply seek excitement, mind games, constant challenges, emotional and financial stress, these personalities below are especially for you.

These types of women claim to be independent, strong, genuine, reasonable, spiritual/religious, and fair, but in actuality, they are all skeezers seeking to take advantage of a good man's time, resources and/or finances.

They are pretenders, hypocrites, hustlers, liars when it comes to interaction with a good man. Many of them may do well or pretend to be doing well when they don't have a man in their life but when it comes to interacting with a good man, they will eventually or immediately dump their financial and physical responsibilities onto him.

There is no legitimate reason why any good man should waste his time with these types of women. These types of women have made poor choices in their lives, are now paying the price for it and looking for a good, suckerman to bail them out.

You are officially notified that these skeezers are in your city now or coming soon to you.

A skeezer can have multiple personalities and are experts at deceit. These females should be left to the players that they truly deserve.

Skeezers do not like good men having a healthy relationship with their mothers because just as animals have that ability to smell fear mothers have that ability to smell skeezers. From that point on, moms guards are up and looking out for her son's best interest which skeezers despise.

The following is a list of documented skeezers.

There are many undocumented ones that are roaming the world posing as good women seeking to take advantage of good and naive men and dump their responsibilities onto them.

There are good, responsible women out there with and without children seeking companionship and not a male to assume their responsibilities.  Don't settle for less!!

It is your personal responsibility and your moral obligation to inform as many men that you know the whereabouts of any skeezer and to avoid them whenever possible.  If you don't avoid them then blame no one but you for the eventual pain and suffering that will come to you.

**PIGEON** – She lives by the creed, "The more men I meet, the more free meals I should be able to eat".  She's always ready to eat and expects a man to pay for her meals no matter how much money she has.  Her attitude is you are the man, you are supposed to do the inviting and whoever invites should pay.

Tell that skeezer you are a man, not her man. This type has no respect for you and seldom invites any male out for dinner. The most that she deserves is a not-so-happy meal so get her one and call it a day.

**DRAMA QUEEN** – If you want nothing else in life but arguments and stress this is the one. The only peace you will get from her is a good piece of ass. She has very little or no self control and is rated number one, two and three when it comes to ignorant and stupid behavior. Her contribution to mankind is going to be stress and sex. They are excellent if you are seeking just a booty call.

She could be a nice display piece, depending on her looks, when you are in public as long as she keeps her mouth shut. Unfortunately, preventing her from saying or doing something stupid in public is almost impossible so use caution if you are going to be seen with her in public places.

Other than having an outside fling, they are quite useless for anything else. These are usually the ones good men fall for most of the time because the sex (when she allows him to have a sample) is off the charts. Her self-esteem is at its highest while engaging in sex or arguing with you.

**BEGGA LOTT** – She is usually financially over-extended due to her immature financial behavior. She is unable to pay her bills most of the time and expects you to pay or is able to pay and just expects you to pay them anyway. She sometimes will agree to break you off a piece in return but make sure you get yours before or as soon as you pay because you may not get yours after you pay.

**INDEPENDENT** – She plays the independent game well. She has a job (or self-employed), car, an apartment (or house), claims independence and will openly express that she doesn't need a man's money. Go out on dates with her and see if she pays for her so-called independent self. Typically she will say "well, he offered to pay," so don't offer and see if she pays and stays. Most of these women require men to make more money than they to eventually support their lifestyle.

This type usually discriminates based upon your financial or social status and will not accept you if she thinks or knows you are below that status.

There is a very good chance that these women are over-extended financially and would only be a liability to you. The more money that they earn, the more money, credit card debt, etc. they will spend and will eventually expect you to help bail them out.

**HOLY ROLLER** – She is saved and waiting on the Lord to send her that mate, but all you have to do is attend church regularly, dress in nice suits so she can be seen with you and accepted by her church peers, spend a little money on her and she will be the biggest freak you ever had before marriage and will justify it by saying that God sent you to her. She possibly has moved from one church to another or one city to another after sexing those so-called God sent men which include ministers and deacons.

**HOLY HUSTLER** – She is the hypocritical and psychologically disturbed twin sister of Ms Holy Roller. She speaks of herself as being prominent in her church and community. She claims that she is a very spiritual person and will present a model image to the members in her church and community to conceal her other personality.

The other personality is a coldhearted hustler and user of any man that she can take advantage of. She worships material items, cash and the desire of a lavish lifestyle by way of the bible and is quite skilled in using the "God Game" to acquire cash, assets, favors, etc., from men, and use that same "God Game" to keep good men at a safe, non-sexual but manipulative distance "In The Name of HER Lord and Savior Jesus Christ."

**PACKAGE DEAL** – This is Ms. So Fine and good looking that in the past when she had no children she would not give the good man the chance at a relationship. Now, with that package on her hip, she will say, "I made a mistake."

Years later and being unable to attract the same kind of men that knocked her up, she is ready to settle down with the types of men she ignored in the past. Are you ready to pay for this package?

What she did was submit to men she thought was exciting and appeared to have money or social status and got knocked up one or several times.

Chances are if she did not smell the scent of financial relief in you or was younger and without that package, she would still never give you the time of day. As long as her packages are still with her, she may still have that emotional bond with the father or fathers. Most of these types tend to never let go emotionally from those fathers unless you will be willing to accept her, her package and all of the responsibilities that comes with her.

Notice her feet are pointing inward, the knees and thighs are wedged together. In most cases, that means the ONLY playing you will get consistently is playing daddy to the children, baby sitting, buying toys and consistently providing services and finances to help support her and another man's children while the father or fathers are out there enjoying life the way you should be doing.

**GOLD DIGGER** – A closet prostitute that insists you pay for the dates if you want to be with her. She typically juggles more than one man at a time and now with the internet, she's a cyber ho. Bring your credit card, cash and condoms in case you get lucky, don't think you are the only one she is seeing and leave your heart at home. Her philosophy is life is too short to be around men that cannot afford her desired lifestyle.

**PLAYING HARD TO GET** (TEASE) – For the man that wants nothing in life but wasted time because this one lives for the attention only.

She knows from first contact if she does or does not have a physical attraction to you and enjoys keeping you in suspense. She will let you get just close enough to keep you around to cater to her and stroke her ego.

**PARTY GIRL** – She lives in the world of fantasy, fun & recreation. Typically, she is the young cutie that's looking for a man or men that will allow her to continue to live that irresponsible, carefree lifestyle. What she refuses to see is that with time and receiving all the attention, she will go from that "young, firm cutie" to that "ole', loose booty call" that no one will commit to.

**WILL NOT CALL** – Collecting phone numbers to her is all a game. The mentality is to take your number to simply get rid of you. In most cases she will not call you. Do not give her your number unless she gives you hers. If both of you have a cell phone don't give her your number. Ask her for her number so that you can call her right now and it will be placed in her caller ID. If she, for any reason, refuses to give you her number then she has no intent in calling you. Simply move on and away from her and do not give her your number hoping she will call because she won't unless she wants to use you.

**N. DEE NILE** (WAITING FOR EX) – Here is the classic case of being in denial. She is waiting on an ex because the look, sex and/or money were too good to let go of and she wants only him. Do not place any emotion into her because he or they may be periodically making a booty call or spending a little time with her to make sure she does not go to you or someone else. She will not tell them no, will kick you to the curb or put you on hold as soon as she gets her recall notice. See her as they do which is simply a booty call when opportunity permits.

**WAITED TOO LONG** – She waited years to exhale with him and eventually the man she waited on exhaled with another woman.

These types usually develop that cougar mentality. They become bitter, develop an attitude and will start dating younger men. Some may even get pregnant to trap the younger man into marriage. Many will claim that getting pregnant was a mistake. In reality she is lying to herself and others.

The younger man will have a good time "spanking that ole ass" and receiving the gifts, money, etc. because to him it's a means to an end (i.e., money, gifts, services, etc) from her. He will get, if he doesn't already have, a younger woman on the side that turns him on physically for his sexual pleasure.

Once the younger male matures to a certain age and state of mind, he will begin to put forth his attention and efforts towards women younger than he and will toss that (or those) ole cougars back into the recycle bin for males younger than he to play with or simply leave them for the older males they rejected in their past.

## Chapter 12 - What is that Skeezer Really Thinking?

There are far too many good men so desperate to have a female that they overlook what a skeezer really means when she is speaking to him. There is a difference between a skeezer's statements and her thoughts. I will take just a few of their statements and expose their true thoughts for the good men that aren't capable of doing so or they are in denial and won't accept reality.

Skeezer's Words:

I would like for us to try and be friends first.

Skeezer's Thoughts:

I am not physically attracted to you so I would like to see how much use you would be to me before I decide if I want to keep you around me.

Skeezer's Words:

I like you but I don't want to ruin our friendship.

Skeezer's Thoughts:

I have no physical interest in you. I like what you do for me (no sex of course) so I want to keep you at a distance just in case I do meet someone that I want to get physical with.

Skeezer's Words:

I can't find a good man.

Skeezer's Thoughts:

I don't want you and I can't get the men that I choose to stop treating me like crap.

Skeezer's Words:

I don't have any single girlfriends.

Skeezer's Thoughts:

I have single girlfriends but not any that I would introduce to you.

Skeezer's Words:

I don't like a cheap man.

Skeezer's Thoughts:

If you want to spend time with me you will have to spend your money on me.

Skeezer's Words:

I would like someone who is very intelligent.

Skeezer's Thoughts:

You should earn a large enough income to be spent on me.

Skeezer's Words:

I would like someone who is very sweet.

Skeezer's Thoughts:

You should want me so badly that you will do anything for me.

Skeezer's Words:

I would like someone who is very romantic.

Skeezer's Thoughts:

You should provide me with that fantasy life-style I desire.

Skeezer's Words:

I would like someone who is respected.

Skeezer's Thoughts:

You should be admired by others so that it lifts my low self-esteem being with you.

Skeezer's Words:

I would like someone who is very generous.

Skeezer's Thoughts:

You should give me gifts, money, pay my bills and support my desired lifestyle.

Skeezer's Words:

I would like someone who is spiritual.

Skeezer's Thoughts:

I have no idea what the hell this means but it sounds good saying it.

Skeezer's Words:

I will not have sex until after I am married.

Skeezer's Thoughts:

I have dated men, I have had sex with all the men I was attracted to and they still did not marry me so I will make you wait.

Skeezer's Words:

I make and have my own money.

Skeezer's Thoughts:

I am not going to spend my money if I am with you. That is what your money is for.

Skeezer's Words:

I am not interested in shallow men and I do not have friends who are.

Skeezer's Thoughts:

I saw you first and I can't handle rejection. I will never introduce you to any of my girlfriends that you may be attracted to even if there is a mutual attraction. If I can't be happy with you, I will make sure that none of them will be.

## Chapter 13 - She Wants to be Just Friends

Ever hear these words.... *"Let's just be friends"*. That's the ultimate *"I am not attracted to you"* rejection.

It means that woman, if she is single, unattached and available usually has absolutely no physical attraction to you. Now being just friends will be fine if you also have no personal interest in her and will not allow her to waste your time.

I will caution you to not put yourself in denial thinking that she will change her mind about you. If you do that and she is a skeezer you are going to be used by her for her convenience, not yours.

Here is how your can prove whether or not her interest in becoming your friend is genuine. If she claims she wants to be just friends with you and you have agreed, tell her:

A. You want to meet all of her single female friends and she will tell the ones you are attracted to, in yours and their presence, that she has no personal interest in you; she will recommend that the two of you spend some quality time together and that you and she are just friends. If she claims she has no single female friends then you must ask her what are the benefits for you in becoming friends with her (very important).

B. You will not be wasting your time listening to her complain about other men she has an interest in.

C. You will treat her same as your male and other platonic female friends which means you come and go when you please and when there is a problem you want her to get to the point so you can come to a quick solution and not just babble since that is all you are going to get from her.

D. You only do special favors for those that do the same for you and it will not be one-sided.

E. You won't do things for her that you would do for a woman that you are intimately involved with.

F. You won't do things for her that she would expect from a man she is intimately involved with. Tell her to go and get her own man for those things because after all she is your friend and should be able to take honest and direct communication from you.

G. You will not spend money on her or foolishly loan her money. If the two of you go out on a social venture she is to pay her own way.

The things above will eliminate 95 percent of the skeezers out of your life. If she agrees to and abides by those things above then she truly wants to be your friend. If she doesn't, she's a skeezer so dump her and move on. Always remember that there are good women out there who can establish a genuine friendship if that's what you are seeking.

## Chapter 14 - The Klub: They Got Game

These are the men that get the good women most of the time. They are single, engaged, married and the ones that good women are attracted to and later on complain to the good man about. How in the world do they get these good women? They understand and play the game quite well.

If you are frustrated and disappointed with the women you have been interacting with, it's time for a change in your thinking and behavior.

Good women choose the men of the Klub most of the time. Many of these women are attracted to excitement, game and challenge so they tend to see the good man who is predictable, reliable and stable as boring.

NOTE: The primary difference between the Pulpit Pimp and Player is the pimp is usually married and engages in sex with as many outside women for as long as he physically can. If he's married, his wife usually has no problem as long as the cash, big home and lifestyle are there.

**PRINCE CHARMING** – He is a challenge to his own ego and doesn't necessarily want the sex. His objective is to stroke his ego by making as many women possible fall for his charm. He knows that most women are easily susceptible when it comes to flowers, cards, dinners and lots of attention. After he's gotten that egotistical orgasm he will move on to the next conquest leaving her in that void until he returns or until another one comes along with better game.

**COUCH POTATO** – He initially will give her the attention she craves and after he has gotten her hooked he moves his attention to the television, food and couch. He will periodically give in to her requests or demands to change his behavior only long enough to shut her up and have her hopeful that he will remain that way. Women considered him to be not as physically attractive as other men, think they would have him all to themselves without other women trying to steal him and have plans of changing him to suit their needs.

**SUGAR DADDY** – He has a few women that he regularly visits. He does not want a commitment and is only looking for a good time and will pay for it. Typically he looks for the woman 15 to 20 years younger than he and considers a woman his age too old for him. He may have one or several affordable women on his rotation, has no plans on marriage and from time to time will recycle one or a few of them for some younger meat. Once they become a physical, emotional or financial burden it's time for a replacement. He knows they are there for the money and has enough game to flash the cash but keep most of it out of their grubby hands.

**PULPIT PIMP** (The President of the Klub; the Top Dog) - He has the best game in the Klub. He uses religion as his game of choice and will seek women that have no man in their life. He realizes that most of those women will be more loyal to him than to their own man. Women are addicted to his social and financial status and are literally standing in line waiting for their chance to allow him to lay hands and whatever else he wants on them to bless them and spiritually comfort them. He typically will have a wife that probably knows about his game but is not giving up the material perks, ego stroke and envy from other women so she accepts his behavior.

He receives regular sacrificial offerings of tits and ass on the side. He's the only member that gets the quick cash and spanks that ass without effort. His behavior is not considered criminal and if he is caught he knows that all he has to do is ask for forgiveness and it shall be done.

He is the smoothest operator in the Klub and even the Player's game is not as tight as his game.

**PLAYER** – He is quite skilled at the game and loves it, although he can't compete with the Pulpit Pimp. Some Players have converted to the pulpit to get that quick cash and freely spank that ass whenever they want to. The Player sees it all as a sport and is usually the quicker thinker in the Klub. He knows all of the lines and is skilled at reading a woman's body language. The Player knows when to quit and will only take his game so far. If he does not get the results that he is looking for, he moves on to the next one.

**MAMA'S BOY** – He targets the lesser attractive women knowing that they will take care of him and allow him to live off of them. He tells them what they want to hear and even though they know he is lying they still take care of him. He has no problem acquiring the lesser attractive women and will usually have at least three of them on the rotation even if he lives with one of them. The mama's boy does not want to leave home and simply prefers the security that his parent(s) provide; therefore, he will usually leave home only if he finds a woman that will support him financially.

**GIGOLO** – He targets women at least seven years older for him to increase his chances of success and many times he does not ever find her to be physically attractive. He knows that older women love to show him off and brag about him to men her age or older and so he works it to his advantage. He will do what she wants, how she wants it, and how many times she wants it and she will provide money and goods to him.

He doesn't think about how she can satisfy him sexually because he will typically have a younger woman or two available. He knows she is usually lonely, angry about her failed relationship(s) and starving for attention so he will be a good lover, a good listener and agree with what she has to say. In doing so, he knows she will put out as much sex as he can handle as well as reward him with gifts and money. His primary reason for being there is to get paid and not get laid. Sex is a bonus to him, not a requirement or expectation.

**HANDY MAN** – He is usually the strong, muscular buck that females love to see. He is very good at conversation and repairing things and will target women in need of a man with his skills.

He is comfortable with approaching females and does it on a regular basis. His intent is to make them aware of his handyman skills and get them to take his number just in case he is needed.

If she is attracted to him she will accept his phone number and eventually make a service request call. If he does a thorough job he will get paid and possibly laid at that time or a later time. She will eagerly find more work for him or create a situation to have him over so that she can be fixed again.

**PROCRASTINATOR** – He talks about plans that he will never accomplish. He is a master "bull shitter" and the best liar and pretender in the Klub. He talks about plans that give her images of money, excitement and a lavish lifestyle.

This is done to warm women up and get their defenses down. He knows he is a beast in bed and once he performs his masterful, **SEX**orcism technique on her, she will totally submit to him.

He is attractive enough to her such that she willingly accepts his bullshit just long enough for him to get in and unleash that beast. She will become overwhelmed with his stellar performance so when she begins to question his big plans, he will simply unleash that beast upon her again and that will satisfy her for another unspecified period of time.

**WON`T LET GO** – He targets the more insecure and lesser attractive women due to his own insecurities and low self-esteem. He will be extremely attentive, in the beginning, which he knows women love. He will not commit and remain close enough to keep her from committing to another man.

**DOWN LOW (DL)** – He is confident, physically fit, very neat and organized, works out in the gym regularly and can hold a conversation just as long as any woman can and has no problem spending money on women. Many of them are usually in a marital or non-marital, heterosexual relationship and is involved sexually with another or other men.

**WANNA BE PLAYER (FOOL)** – There is always an exception to every rule and this fool is the exception. He thinks that he is a player and will spend lots of money on women. He has lots of imagination and desire but **NO** game, **NO** drive and **NO** balls when it comes to initiating intimate moves. He does not realize skeezers recognize his weakness and lack of game. They will break him emotionally as well as financially and then dump him if a bigger fool or real player comes along and runs a better game on her.

# Chapter 15 - Busy is Just an Excuse

Life is measured in and expires with time. Life is precious and time is irreplaceable because time is life and as time goes so does your life.

If you value your life then don't foolishly waste time waiting for or wanting a woman that does not value you. Since time waits for no one, why would you foolishly do so?

When a woman tells you she is too busy and is not available that means one of two things:

She has very little or no time for socializing due to her other obligations,

She does not value you enough to make time for you.

Busy means full of activity and unavailable means not capable of being used or seen. We all have activity in our lives but for most it's "activity with no productivity" which means many of us are expending a lot of time producing nothing.

Busy (activity) is a necessity if one is to produce something so if you aren't active, you really aren't producing a thing. Unavailable, in most cases, is simply a choice that one makes. Only a very minute group of people are so busy that they are not available. They just choose to be unavailable for you because they don't value you so come out of denial, accept it and move on.

The next time you have an interest in a woman and she tells you that she "is too busy" or "is not available" simply turn and walk away. If she truly is too busy you will never have enough time to get to know her. There will only be just enough time to spend money on her and then back to her busy life. Is that what you are looking for?

Women have sacrificed their future and their children's future many times for men that they valued that openly did not give a crap about them. So why don't she have time for you? It doesn't matter. She doesn't so just move on.

Accept the unspoken fact she is saying, "She does not value you". This is my suggestion:

**DON'T** get angry at her

**DON'T** de-value yourself as she has done you by sitting around waiting for her to have time for you

**DON'T** try to convince her to spend time with you

**DON'T** question why she don't have time because I have already told you why

**DON'T** make yourself available for her since she isn't doing it for you

**DON'T** allow her or yourself to make excuses for not spending time with you

**DO** move on and away from her mentally and physically **IMMEDIATELY**

**DO** value yourself and know that other women out there will value you

**DO** get out of denial thinking that she is interested in you and does value you

**DO** not think that you can just be friends if you have a personal interest in her

**DO** question her availability motives. She may not value you and is just killing time with you. You will be dumped eventually.

# Chapter 16 - The Key to Peace of Mind

The key to peace of mind, productivity & longevity is cleansing. Take some quality time to evaluate your life and dispose of the toxic waste in your life. I am speaking of the people and things that drain your time, resources and finances.

If you don't go through this cleansing process then shut up, stop complaining about those toxic people or things, accept the drain and drama that they bring and don't burden others with your waste that you choose to not let go of.